RICKY GOES HOME

RICKY GOES HOME

David Newark

XULON PRESS

Xulon Press
2301 Lucien Way #415
Maitland, FL 32751
407.339.4217
www.xulonpress.com

© 2020 by David Newark

All rights reserved solely by the author. The author guarantees all contents are original and do not infringe upon the legal rights of any other person or work. No part of this book may be reproduced in any form without the permission of the author. The views expressed in this book are not necessarily those of the publisher.

Printed in the United States of America.

ISBN-13: 978-1-6305-0326-0

Table of Contents

1. Death Valley 1
2. Ricky's Rehab 4
3. Hidden Pictures 9
4. Big Mike's Aunt Martha 11
5. Ricky's Birthday 14
6. Ricky and Mary's First Date 16
7. Why Not 19
8. Mary Prepares for Ricky (Big Mike) 21
9. Big Mike's First Day Home 25
10. The Real Ricky Wakes Up 27
11. Why the Basement Door
    Was Locked 30
12. Memories 33
13. Ricky Can Be Heard from
    the Basement 36
14. Big Mike Moves in with Mary 39
15. Big Mike's Parents 41

16. Big Mike's School Days 46
17. The Day Mike's Best Friend,
   Buck, Died. 55
18. Big Mike's Nightmares 63
19. The Letter. 66
20. Ricky's Childhood Tree Fort 70
21. Mary Has a Surprise 78
22. Mary Goes into Labor 81
23. The Truth 83
24. Evening News Report 87

1

DEATH VALLEY

Ricky was a twenty-six-year-old marine who had been serving in Iraq for seven years. Three years earlier, on a Christmas leave, he and his wife, Mary, conceived a child, and they named him Chris. Since he was still serving in Iraq, Ricky had never seen his child except through pictures. It was late August, and Ricky was so excited to surprise Mary and Chris for Christmas this year, which would be extra special because his second tour would be over in December, and he was coming home for good.

It was a week before his leave, and he was on a late evening sweep through a part of the city known as Death Valley, as the soldiers would call it. Death Valley was a two-mile stretch of what had once been the most beautiful part of the city. It was next to a river and had shops up and down both sides of the street, and on the sidewalks were fruit and vegetable vendors. Everything was lovely, from the bright yellow bananas to the baskets of the green and purple grapes, with the smell of flowers sold on one corner to the food cooking on the other. That wasn't the case anymore, as the buildings were crushed in half, and not a window was left. Death Valley was gray and black, and the only yellow was the flames from burning building and the cars on the road. The black smoke was so thick that at times, you couldn't see ten feet in front of you. One day the streets are clean, and the next day there's another car bombing—it seems like this happens daily. The soldiers would do evening shifts, after fighting all day to recover bodies from both sides of this terrible war. The smell of food and flowers had been replaced with the smell of burnt rubber and flesh. Their job was to keep the road cleaned so they could get supplies to their base, but the street was never clean.

As they were on their last hour, finishing up with a team of six, Ricky, while leading the team, yelled back, "All is clear. Let's go home, boys." Suddenly, a shot rang out, and Ricky took a direct hit in the head. The soldiers scrambled to look for where the shots had come from so they could return fire, but the streets were silent. As they ran to Ricky's side, they saw a gaping hole in the side of his head, but Ricky was still alive. The soldiers pulled back and rushed Ricky back to the base.

2

RICKY'S REHAB

One week later, Ricky returned home, but not to what was really his home. Ricky was placed in a rehab center, and he had been there for the past five years with TBI (Traumatic Brain Injury). Ricky's son, Chris, was now eight years old and had still never seen his dad. Five years earlier, Mary decided that it would probably not be good for Chris to see his dad in his condition. She has not been back to the rehab center and she couldn't bear the sight of the man she knew and loved. For Mary, her situation resulted not in a "stand by your man" question, but a "God, where is my man" question.

The only living member on Ricky's side of the family was his mom, Linda. When Ricky was a young boy, his dad, Ricky Sr., went missing one day and was never found. Since Ricky was Linda's only son, she could never give up on him. She finally decided to take Chris to see his dad, who was a superhero to Chris. On the ride to the rehab center, Chris talked so much about what he was going to say to his dad. He couldn't stop talking about the things that he and his dad were going to do. "One day, me and dad are going to go fishing and to the park." Chris wanted to go to a park by his house where his mom would take him, where he would see other kids playing with their dads.

As Chris and Linda were walking down the hall to Ricky's room, they arrived at Ricky's closed door, both staring at it. Tears began to run down Linda's face. As she quickly wiped them off, she changed her mind and said to herself, *This is not what I should do.* Ricky had been in a bed by the window, looking out all day, not knowing anyone for the past five years, including his mom. Linda was thinking that if, by some miracle, Chris could see his dad, Ricky would remember that he had a child, even though he had never seen him before. For years, Linda had been waiting for this day until Chris was old enough to understand.

After the drive over and hearing little Chris talk, Linda thought, *No way. I have already lost Ricky (and he doesn't even know he is lost).* She wasn't about to lose little Chris to the traumatic shock of seeing his dad in this condition.

Just as she grabbed Chris's hand to turn around to leave, Chris pulled away from her, opened the door, and ran into the room and to the bedside. "Dad, Dad!" Chris shouted, grabbing and crawling halfway on the bed, feet dangling over the side and arms tightly wrapped around his neck. Crying, he said, "I love you, Dad."

Linda had still not entered the room. With her back against the wall beside the doorway, she heard, "I love you too, son." As Linda looked up, she turned the corner and rushed into the room. She was shocked to see that Ricky had a roommate in the other bed, beside whom Chris was standing, holding on so tightly. With the curtain closed to the other bed, Chris had never even seen Ricky.

Linda couldn't say a word. How could she? How could she break Chris's heart. She wiped the tears from her face, letting it go on. Soon, Linda turned around and saw a name tag on a chalkboard that said "Mike." Before Chris could see, she wiped off the name and removed the pictures and newspaper clippings on the wall—clippings about "Big Mike" holding world records of being the strongest man and other Olympic-looking events. She blocked them from Chris's view by pulling the curtain around. She was about to apologize to Big Mike and explain herself, but she saw that Mike was going right along with it. *Maybe he is playing around,* she thought. *What harm could it be?* She did not think that Chris would want to come back again.

Big Mike looked just like Ricky—muscular, black hair, and about five-foot-seven. As they finished visiting and after Chris filled him in with all the things he had done at school and the hobbies he liked at home, Chris began telling him about Mary and how excited she was going to be. "We are going to have to go and let your dad rest," Linda told Chris. Chris says goodbye and started to leave the room. "Goodbye, Ricky," Linda said, knowing the man's name was Mike. Big Mike spoke up. "I love you. Goodbye."

3

Hidden Pictures

Week after week, Linda and Chris returned to the rehab center. Linda had taken a motherly role with Big Mike, which gave her a comfort that she hadn't felt in a long time, as she felt like part of her son was back, when really, he was behind the curtain in the next bed. She never let Chris into the room first. Linda told him that she needed to go in and make sure his dad was properly dressed. She would even take a large picture from Ricky's side of the room and place it over Big Mike's pictures and newspaper clippings before Chris would enter the room. The picture she would move was one of Ricky during his school days or one of him and Mary's wedding day, but she would never put up any of him being a solider. Linda never wanted to see or talk about the sacrifice she and her family had made.

4

BIG MIKE'S AUNT MARTHA

Big Mike also had TBI, but he was on a comeback. He didn't have any brothers or sisters and no kids, although he always wanted them but had never found a wife. He never took time out of his life to slow down, as he was always training hard for the next event, setting impossible tasks for himself and always overcoming them. Big Mike didn't even know that he had been in a car accident. He once had many friends, but after the first few years of his accident, when the cameras stopped flashing, the people he thought were his friends stopped coming to see him. A forgotten name was all he became. It is hard to believe that you can have so many people say they love you and will be there when you need them, and one day you can wake up alone. In Big Mike's case, he did not remember them anyway, so it was no loss to him.

Linda had learned all of this from reading the newspaper clips and talking with the nurses at the rehab center, who said Big Mike's only living relative was his Aunt Martha. She was a prayer warrior, and she prayed day after day at his bedside. Aunt Martha was alone in life—no kids, no husband…I guess you could call her somewhat of a nun, but the love she gave was like no other.

At the age of eighty-seven, after the year she lost her little sister, Big Mike's mom, Aunt Martha passed away in her sleep the same day Big Mike woke up from his coma, one year and twenty-three days after his accident. People said it seemed like whatever she prayed for, God answered, and I am sure she was praying for Big Mike to wake up; he did the day she died.

Big Mike is a world famous superhero, a strong man holding titles that say he is the strongest in the world. Yet after weeks turned into months of rehab, Big Mike's body went from 312 pounds of rock hard muscle to 180 pounds of mush. The muscles in his stomach had been so strong that the surgical tools could not cut his stomach. The doctors had to call maintance at the hospital to get a circular saw to get through the muscle. It was touch and go for Big Mike, whose fans and competitors had called him Giant Killer.

One Wednesday, when Big Mike was at therapy, Linda was able to get Ricky out of the room to take him down to the church service held at the rehab center without Big Mike knowing it. Each Sunday, she would return to take Big Mike down with Chris. She had been doing this for so long, and she was so caught up in the lie she was living that she didn't even call him Big Mike anymore; both were so out of it due to TBI that they probably wouldn't know what was going on anyway. At the church services, Linda would always ask for forgiveness inside herself for what she was doing, and from time to time, she would be mad at God and blamed Him while trying to justify her lie.

5

RICKY'S BIRTHDAY

One Wednesday, Linda and Ricky were at the prayer service. It was a special day because it was Ricky's birthday, and the service that day had anointing with oil. The pastor read a verse from the book of James chapter 5, asking, "If anyone of you are sick, let them seek the elders of the church to anoint them with oil, and they shall be healed."

"No harm in that," Linda said to herself. "Ricky won't ever be healed, but maybe somehow God will bless his soul—that is, if there is even a soul in there." Linda always felt convinced that she was trying to make things right, trying to be God in some sort of way to bring love to her grandson and Big Mike. She wanted to make everyone's life better.

That day, the rehab center church was full as people were gathered singing and praising God, laying hands on others and anointing them with oil. Then came Ricky's turn. The people prayed, "Lord, we pray that in three years, Ricky will go home and be healed." At that moment, Linda was living in a daydream. The Spirit was moving, and tears of happiness and joy surpassing all understanding fell down her face. As quickly as it had started, the service ended, and Linda pushed Ricky back to his room, knowing that in his mind, he had probably never left.

6

RICKY AND MARY'S FIRST DATE

Chris and Big Mike were bonding so much you could not separate them. It now seemed like Big Mike was his new dad. Chris still couldn't stop talking to Mike about his mom, Mary. Mary was still not ready to see her husband, for she was broken knowing that all the memories they had were erased from Ricky's mind.

Mary lived in a small house down the street from Linda. Linda's house was quite large, with two stories and a basement. Chris spent most of his time in the attic bedroom, which felt like the third floor to Chris. With the window open and the cool breeze at night, Chris felt like he was closer to the stars. That was where he would talk to God.

Mary was a real estate agent, and she worked most of the weekends, when her clients were mostly off work and could view properties. Mary never divorced Ricky; from time to time, she dated, but no man could win her heart. She always longed for Ricky and compared everyone to him.

Ricky and Mary's first date was at the fair. Ricky was a little shorter then Mary, but his arms were so strong. He had been head of the weightlifting team at school. Mary was petite, with long brown hair that looked golden when the sunlight hit it. Most schoolmates called them Ken and Barbie. At the fair booths, Ricky would win all the games, from the sledgehammer bell to the baseball bottle breaking, right down to the little kissing booth. It was a dollar for a kiss and a picture of the pretty girl, but when Ricky pulled out $20, Mary felt threatened. The girl was so pretty, but to this day, she thought Ricky had it planned out. With Ricky's eyes closed, the girl walked out from behind the booth, pulling Mary and pushing her into Ricky. Ricky's eyes opened, and Mary just knew that it had been planned all along. That kissed lasted a long time, and Ricky's arms wrapped around her. She never forgot that memory.

7

WHY NOT

Finally, the day when Big Mike was able to be released came, but he would have to have a caretaker, since he had no wife and no family. Big Mike lost his mom and dad in the car accident. He was the only survivor, and to the day of his release, he didn't even remember his past. He thought Linda was his mom, and he believed Chris was his son and Mary was his wife.

It had been so many years since Mary had seen Ricky that she had almost forgotten what he looked like. Mary didn't know about the lie Linda had been telling, and to make it worse, the administrator of the rehab center had asked Linda if she would take Big Mike home to be his caretaker. Linda slept on it for a couple of days. It had been almost three years since that prayer had been prayed over Ricky's life, and Linda was starting to think that somehow God put Big Mike into her life to maybe rebuild Ricky's family. Linda knew what Mary and Chris had been going through for years. She asked God, "Do I take Big Mike home to live Ricky's life? Is that what You had planned? He is like a dad to Chris, and people adopt family and kids all the time." Linda sat there for a few blank minutes waiting, as if God was just going to speak up with a loud voice and say yes or no. Then Linda said to herself, "Why not?"

8

Mary Prepares for Ricky (Big Mike)

Linda decided to take Big Mike home. He had been called Ricky since the day Chris had met him. Linda had successfully hidden all the signed paperwork from the rehab center and the newspaper clippings and pictures in Big Mike's room of his past life. His name was now Ricky.

Ricky's wife, Mary, was not ready for this day. She had thought that it was impossible, but her son had been updating her about all the improvements over the past few years. Mary began dreaming of the day Ricky would come home for his home visit from the service. She saw Ricky come down the walkway at the airport, dressed in his camo clothes.

For a short man, he was standing tall, but when Mary had her arms around him and he wrapped his around her, she remembered that extra tug that he would always give. It was a special thing that only they knew about, just two small squeezes and then the big one… bump, bump, bam. That's the hug that Mary remembered.

Mary had not dated in a year or so, since she knew her husband was coming home. Feeling guilty for cheating on him and not seeing him, she pleaded for God's forgiveness at the side of her bed, where she and Ricky used to lay. The bed was special—they had picked it out together, and it was the first piece of furniture they bought for their house; no other man had ever slept in it. It was a California King made of cherry wood with four big posts and iron rods crossing the top—beautiful. The posts were as big as small trees, and there was brown leather padding on the headboard and footboard. The pillows said "His and Hers" to show which side they each slept on, but the blanket said "Together Forever." Until that day, Mary had kept them in the closet for years. Mary knew Ricky had problems, but she couldn't wait to see him and be in his arms again. She put on her best dress after making up the bed and pillows.

Linda had planned a big home-cooked meal for Ricky at her house. Mary headed down the street to Linda's, about a block away on the other side of the street. When Mary got to Linda's house, Chris was already there from staying over the night before. Linda was not yet home with Ricky. Mary and her son hung up banners saying "Welcome Home, Dad," and signs saying "Welcome Home, Hero," which were well overdo, lined the street for blocks. Everything was ready, and they couldn't think of anything that was missing except friends and family.

"We must have the smallest family on earth," Chris said. Mary laughed. "You're probably right," she said. Long ago, Mary's family moved away to Oklahoma, where she and Chris visit every other year.

The year Linda's husband went missing, her neighbors Ray and Nancy, who were best friends, stopped coming over. Nancy had worked with Linda for many years. Linda had been an elementary school teacher until she lost her first child, Laurie, as a toddler. After taking some time off work, she decided to change to middle school, so she would not have to bear the sight of little ones. But middle school was no relief. Linda could not stop thinking of the young adult Laurie may have become. She became so cold and angry that no one wanted to be around her. Christmas time was extra hard on Linda until the day Ricky was born. She felt that God had blessed her life again. A year or so after Laurie's passing, Ray and Nancy also moved.

9

BIG MIKE'S
FIRST DAY HOME

Finally, Linda's van came up the driveway. Ricky was home—where he had been raised as a child. As the front door of the house flew open, Chris came running toward the van that hadn't even parked yet. "Dad, dad!" he yelled. Ricky's window was up, and he was not even out of the car yet when Chris got the first hug.

Mary met Ricky halfway down the sidewalk, seeing him for the first time in almost ten years. She looked at him twice but didn't think for another minute; she opened her arms as Ricky opened his. "You're so beautiful," he said. With that hug and her chin on Ricky's shoulder, Mary was crying, waiting and waiting for that special hug. But it was not the same, and she realized nothing was. She cried a little harder, knowing that his mind was still not all there yet. Mary put off bringing Ricky to her house that night. For now, she knew Linda had to care for him 24/7, since Mary was working a lot. Linda's house was all set up for Ricky.

Mary had kept her house, thinking Ricky would one day come back home. Chris had a bedroom at both Linda's and Mary's houses, but he stayed with Linda a lot due to his mom's work schedule. Mary decided to clean out one of her rooms at her house to set up a home office so that she could be closer to Ricky and her son. It had only been six months since Big Mike—"Ricky"—had been home.

10

THE REAL RICKY WAKES UP

This was a special day—it was Ricky's birthday and the three-year mark of Ricky's anointing prayer service he and Linda had at the rehab center. Since she had taken Big Mike home, Linda didn't come to see her son as much anymore. Ricky had been on a feeding tube for eleven years and didn't talk.

Then, on a Wednesday service, as the staff was feeding the elders donuts and coffee and singing songs, a nurse walked by Ricky. He said, "Hey, I am hungry—starving! Can I get something to eat?" Ricky finally woke up to the world. He didn't remember his past, but he remembered things like food, clothes, and pieces of life—but that was enough to start life over again.

The rehab center called Linda to tell her that they had news about Ricky. "Can you please hold while the administrator gets on the other line?" they said. On the phone, Linda's life flashed back to the day she had held that phone when the doctors told her about Laurie, and she started to cry. Then she heard the administrator's voice: "Linda, I have to tell you something. I don't know how or why..." Instantly, Linda's mind slipped into a deja vu, thinking those were the exact words she had heard before. Then she heard that Ricky had woken up.

"What do you mean?" she said, not understanding what the administrator was saying. He told her Ricky was talking and eating. "I will be right there," Linda said, hanging up the phone and telling Chris and Big Mike she would be right back. Mary was not at the house, as she was out picking up gifts for Ricky's—Big Mike's—birthday.

As Linda drove to the rehab center, she was afraid. She had dug herself so deep into the lie she has been living that she didn't know how she was going to get out of it, and she knew she probably couldn't.

As she visited the administrator and Ricky, they explained to her that he didn't have memory of his past or his condition and that he would have to be taught these aspects of his life again. Knowing what Linda had done with Big Mike's recovery, she believed she could do this. No one knew the lie Linda had been living. As she was there with Ricky for his birthday, she couldn't stop thinking about what she should do. Looking up from time to time, she prayed, "God, please help me. I can't get out of this one, and he is my son."

Then, as she left the rehab center and began her way back home, Linda's mind started wandering. Big Mike was living Ricky's life, and Mary was back with her husband and Chris. *Oh, my Chris. I don't know what to do,* Linda thought.

After a week went by, Linda had come up with a plan. She decided to sneak her real son, Ricky, into the basement that she had set up like a studio apartment. It would be just like the rehab center Ricky had lived in all those years.

11

Why the Basement Door Was Locked

The basement door at Linda's house was always locked. This was due to an incident many years ago, right before Laurie turned three years old. Laurie was going down the basement stairs when she fell, breaking both her legs. She was put in a full-body cast from the chest down. This happened around Christmas, and the doctors and the nurses were so nice to her. They painted her cast like a candy cane, even giving her a teddy bear and putting the same candy cane cast on the teddy bear. Their kindness was so loving and heartwarming. The doctors said Laurie was going to make a full recovery, but it was going to be a long one. Then, around midnight that night, Linda went home to get some clothes to stay the night at the hospital, and the phone rang. It was the doctor. He told Linda that he didn't know how or why, but Laurie had passed away. The doctor could not even finish the words "I'm sorry" before Linda had dropped the phone in shock. Life had never been the same for Linda. She almost never recovered from losing Laurie.

A few years later, Linda was pregnant. When she found out it was a boy, she decided to name him Ricky Junior. He was nine pounds with black hair and green eyes, and he looked just like his dad. Linda's husband, Ricky Senior, was a fisherman who would spend a couple of months at a time out at sea. The last day Linda had seen her husband, she and little Ricky saw him off at the dock. She baked him an upside-down pineapple cake and made cupcakes for the crew. Linda also got Ricky Senior a new button-up captain shirt with a name tag that said "Captain Ricky Senior."

As a kid, Ricky had never played in or had seen the basement. No one did—no one was to ever go down there, and they were not even to question it. They all knew the story of Ricky's sister, and that door stayed locked.

12

MEMORIES

Every weekend, Mary had Big Mike at her and Chris's house, so Linda would get to spend time with her son, Ricky, in her basement. She would also sneak in at night throughout the week. The weeks and months turned into years. As time went by, Ricky became better and better, saying things like he couldn't wait to get back to work fishing on his boat. These statements were so touching for Linda, as they brought her back to her husband. Ricky Junior's dream had always been to become a fisherman like his dad.

One night, after a week of bad weather on the sea, Linda woke up at home from lighting that had been so close. Somehow, she knew something was different about this storm. The next day, on the news, Linda learned that there was a fishing boat that had capsized and gone missing off the radar, and an SOS and the coastguard went out. With her eyes glued to the TV, she wondered if it was Ricky. There was no news about it for two weeks. The search was called off due to nothing being found, and Ricky's ship never sailed in. "There is no way this could be happening to me," Linda said. She spent all her days and weeks thinking that every phone call would be her husband, but that day never came. Ricky Senior was lost at sea.

Life for Linda wasn't all bad; some of Linda's best times were when Ricky Junior was in middle school. He was in her class, and that's also where Ricky and Linda met Mary, who was also a student in her class. To watch the two of them grow together was more than any mom could ask for.

Linda had the best of both worlds at home and school, from the sports to all the challenges that life had to offer. She was right by Ricky's side.

Ricky always wanted to do more, and he could not face the fact that so many people had fought for his freedom and he had done nothing to repay them for it. After giving it much thought, Ricky decided to join the Marine corps. His mom was not happy, for she knew there was a war going on and a lot of people were losing their lives. Ricky was all she had left. She didn't want to lose him, but she respected his wishes. Ricky was good at everything he did; he was a fighter, and Linda trusted that God would not take Ricky.

Mary was not happy either. She knew, though, that if Ricky didn't go, he would always feel bad about having his freedom and that if he went, he was going to complete it because that was what he did best—finish what he started. So, off to war he was.

As the bus pulled away, there was no turning back, but Ricky looked back to see his mom and Mary. Tears started to form, but he quickly snuffed them out and focused on his new journey.

=13=

RICKY CAN BE HEARD FROM THE BASEMENT

One weekend, Big Mike was visiting Chris and Mary's house down the street. Linda had the door open to the kitchen hallway, which led to the door of the cellar. She saw steam filling up the hallway, thinking it was smoke, when she heard Ricky screaming downstairs. As she rushed down the stairs, she found out that the hot water pipe had broken, and the room was flooded. What she thought was smoke was only steam, but it had set Ricky off into a panic. Shutting the water off, Linda didn't know what to do. She couldn't call a plumber since Ricky was in the basement and she knew that Ricky could be heard if he screamed. Linda knew nothing about plumbing, but she did know about watching videos on the internet, after learning about them during most of Big Mike's rehab. So she started searching for videos on how to fix a hot water pipe.

After calming Ricky down and putting a movie on for him to watch, she finished cleaning up the water. She then made a quick run to the hardware store, being sure to lock the basement door behind her. The whole time she was thinking, *God, I hope he doesn't scream.* While there, she picked up four packs of four-inch Styrofoam, which was all that could fit in her van at the moment.

Her plans were to put the Styrofoam on the back of Ricky's door to soundproof his room. She also decided that it was time to remodel. After watching videos and learning how to do so much, she set up the basement like an apartment. For the first couple of months, the basement had been like rehab center.

Now, after fixing the water pipes, Linda had the idea to start recording everything Big Mike did upstairs, from the birthdays of Chris and the times spent with Mary to Chris's graduation and everything in between. Every night, she would go to the basement, telling Ricky what he did yesterday, which was far from the truth, for Ricky never left the room.

14

BIG MIKE MOVES IN WITH MARY

A little over a year had passed, so Mary finally said to Linda, "It's time to take Ricky home." Mary told Linda that sleeping in their old bed may help him remember things of their past. Linda didn't want Big Mike to remember his past, but she had been working overtime on her real son and thought that Mary's idea was probably best.

Mary had the perfect setting: Big Mike's favorite lasagna and a warm bath with that special pillow and comforter. She had picked out a beautiful evening gown. It was Saturday night, and Chris was staying at Linda's house. All was going well. Mary was talking to Big Mike a lot throughout the night, asking him if he remembered anything. "No, I am sorry," Big Mike said.

Mary said, "It's ok. Give it some time."

After a few weeks went by, one night in their bed, Big Mike was talking in his sleep. He was saying he was going to win. "Win!" he shouted. "Win!" He was a deep sleeper, and it took Mary shaking him a few times to wake him. Her old Ricky had been a light sleeper.

"Are you ok?" Mary asked.

"Yes," Big Mike said. "I was dreaming."

"What about?"

"I was in a contest, and the crowds were cheering me on," Big Mike answered. "I just remember winning something big, but then it went blank and you woke me up."

"I'm sorry," Mary said, "but you scared me."

"It's ok. It's just a dream."

===== 15 =====

BIG MIKE'S PARENTS

Big Mike's mom and dad were named Dee and Gary. Dee was always raised in church, and she had a good upbringing. Gary...not so much. He had to learn about life the hard way. Not that he got in trouble, but he seemed to always have trouble follow him—until he married Dee. Both had a past, and they were much older when they had their son, Big Mike. They were in there forties when Big Mike was born.

Dee had been married to her first husband at a young age, and she had no kids with him. They had tried and prayed for years, but with no luck. Her first husband's name was Danny, and he passed away from cancer, leaving

Dee alone for ten years. She said she would never marry another, but then she met Gary.

As for Gary, he was raised poor, having to work for everything, and he had to fight to keep it. He grew up during a time when if you wanted to get somewhere in life, it wasn't going to be handed to you. The only escape was to join the navy. In the navy, you could see the world and have a good paycheck with health benefits for issues like a simple toothache. The only problem with joining the navy was the war going on in Vietnam. No one wanted to go to this war, but if Gary wanted to leave the life of poverty, he would have to fight.

Gary did his time and served his country, and he was proud of it too. But coming home was even worse than leaving. As Gary stepped off the plane, it was like walking into a different country whose citizens didn't want him there. Outside the airport, crowds were yelling, "Trader!" "Baby killer!" "Hope you burn in hell!" These statements were even posted on signs the crowds were carrying.

While Gary tried to catch a cab to get out of there, the police were blocking the protesters from getting to him. Still, the words hurt him worse than any physical pain man could ever cause.

Finally, Gary got a taxi. As he was pulling away, the driver said, "Not so friendly, are they?"

"No, they're not." said Gary. He knew about the feedback of the war but never really thought it would be this bad.

"Mister, don't take this the wrong way, but you should change them clothes," the driver said. "I don't think you can even get a room at a hotel or eat dinner in this town wearing them."

As Gary looked down at his sleeve and saw his American flag, he shed a tear. "If you could drive me to the next town…I have family there."

After some time, Gary reconnected with an old girlfriend and married her. Her name was Tina. Tina and Gary never had kids, and after many years together, Tina passed away from breast cancer. Gary was broken. He moved back to his hometown in Cordell, Georgia, to take care of his mother. She was alone, as Gary's dad passed away from a heart attack the same year Tina did.

Gary would always stop by a small fruit stand on the edge of town. To his surprise, an old friend, Dee, owned the stand. Dee and Danny had been friends with Gary and Tina. Neither one of them knew about each other's spouse, now seeing each other for the first time in many years.

At the same time, they both said, "How is your wife?" "How is your husband?" With a pause, Gary and Dee smiled at each other, and Gary let Dee tell her story first. He was shocked to hear the news about Danny, and he started to tear up. When Dee saw this, she said, "I'm ok. Gary."

Then Gary told Dee about his wife, Tina. Dee was also shocked and just as sad as he had been. She reached out for a hug. It was the first time each of them felt the love of even just a friend, and that was something special that they both had needed.

They started spending a lot of time together, and their friendship went from small walks in the park to dinners on weekends. Shortly after, Gary asked Dee to marry him. As Dee pondered all her thoughts, she wondered what people would say. She took these thoughts to prayer and remembered those vows—"Till death do us part." Neither one would ever be parted from the memories they had made with their first spouses.

Finally, Dee said yes to Gary's proposal. Then came Big Mike.

16

BIG MIKE'S SCHOOL DAYS

School life for Big Mike wasn't always good to him. On Big Mike's first day at school, he was so happy to finally get to go. His mom and dad had been telling him about how wonderful school was going to be and all the new friends he would make. Being an only child, Big Mike could only follow in his mom and dad's footsteps, so they spoiled him, teaching him everything they could, trying to prepare him for that first day of school.

Big Mike was not dressed for the times. He was wearing tacky pants and a striped shirt, which looked way outdated to the other kids at school. What looked cool for Dee and Gary was way off for Big Mike, which he found out that first day. When Big Mike's parents dropped him off at school for his first day in first grade, his mom and dad walked him into the lunchroom, where all the kids were supposed to meet to sign in for their classrooms. Big Mike had his tacky clothes on, but what stood out the most were his glasses—with tiger-striped frames of green, brown, and some yellow. His choice was black frames. He knew he was not dressed like everyone else.

When Dee finished filling out all the paperwork, she walked over to Big Mike in front of everyone. Then she did the unthinkable—she licked her thumb, then wiped off a piece of chocolate donut from Big Mike's face before kissing him on the cheek. By now, all the kids were laughing at Big Mike.

After his parents left the room, it felt like the whole school was laughing. But then came Carol. She had missed all the fun at Big Mike's expense, but she did take a liking to Big Mike's shoes and outfit.

As everyone was in line to leave the lunchroom, Big Mike experienced his first bully—a boy named Brian. It started with, "Hey, four eyes! Did your grandma and grandpa dress you and drop you off?"

"Hahaha!" It seemed like every eye was on him again. Some of the kids laughing along with Brian seemed to laugh only so they would not be a target for Brian's bullying. You could see the relief on their faces.

Big Mike made it through lunch, then it was time for the playground. Not where Big Mike wanted to be—alone with all the kids with the teacher one hundred yards away, sitting in a chair next to the door. Big Mike was watching most of the kids, mainly Brian. But at the swing set was Carol. She was a small girl with red hair and blue eyes, and wouldn't you know it, she had the same glasses.

Big Mike noticed a big line forming at the end of the monkey bars, at least ten kids deep on each side, with a crowd around it. There was one kid name Arthur, a black boy bigger then Brian, who was challenging Brian on the monkey bars. Brian was a big boy himself, a country boy who would always wear a cowboy hat. The challenge was to climb out to the middle, wrap their legs around each other's waist, and pull the other down, tearing their arms off the monkey bars and making them fall a few feet down. Brian was always beating everyone in line—until Arthur came along, and boy, was Big Mike liking that. The bully was getting what he deserved.

This was all good until Brian saw Big Mike laughing. On Brian's way up from the sand, he grabbed a big handful of it and threw it into Big Mike's face. Everyone stopped to see what Big Mike was going to do about it, but he did nothing. He was sure glad he had glasses on that day because no sand got into his eyes.

As Big Mike walked back to the swings, Carol was sad for him, but she quickly took off his glasses and began to clean them with her shirt. Big Mike had his first girlfriend on the first day of school. He went home happy but sad in some ways because of how he was treated. "I wish I was bigger," he said to himself.

A couple of weeks went by, and Big Mike tried to avoid Brian as much as he could. But it seemed impossible; every day was worse and worse. One day, Big Mike was on the playground thinking to himself, *If I could just beat Arthur at the monkey bars, then I would be the winner and maybe no one would pick on me.*

Each day, he would finish his lunch early and head out to the playground. He did this for a few weeks, practicing hanging on the monkey bars, until he ended up hanging on longer than anybody else. He even made a new challenge: who could hang the longest.

Then, after a few more days, Arthur was hanging on the other end of the monkey bars. Big Mike did not see him get on because he was on his way back to the ladder, but soon a crowd came running over. Big Mike turned around, scared, but he accepted the challenge. They both wrapped their legs around each other so many times—no one could believe how long they were hanging there, not even Brian, who was in the front row. That day, Big Mike found out that the other boys were bigger, but he was stronger. He won the contest, and just like that, the bullying stopped. Carol and Big Mike were together for another year or so.

Big Make was eight years old now and in third grade, and he was on Christmas break. On Christmas Eve, he was waiting for Santa to show up and bring him a new bike, but he knew that baby Jesus was the reason for the season. Santa didn't show up that night, but what did show up was a fire that burned Big

Mike's house to the ground. Everyone made it out, but Big Mike's dad had a heart attack in the driveway. Thankfully, he lived. During that break, Big Mike had to move to an apartment across town and go to a new school, never seeing Carol again.

When he began his new school after Christmas break, he decided not to wear his glasses anymore, taking them off before going in each day. Once again, he was the new kid, and it appeared that he needed to prove himself all over again. The kids weren't so friendly.

The apartment where he lived was located right next to the school. It was a rough part of town, and a railroad track went behind the apartment. Big Mike's first week was ok. His clothes were different, he didn't have glasses, and his mom didn't pay lot of attention to that. She was dealing with his dad's health, so Big Mike was able to get away with things more often.

Big Mike met some new friends: Kevin and Steve. After school, all three of them would walk the tracks behind the apartment building and throw rocks at the railroad bridge. One day, a group of kids came, and a few of them were cousins of Arthur from Big Mike's old school. They knew the story of Big Mike, and Kevin and Steve took that story to school the next day. Big Mike had a bad boy reputation, and it reached the biggest bully, named Jay.

A couple of days went by, and Big Mike and Jay never spoke to each other. Their friends instigated a fight after school on the railroad tracks, which was not what Big Mike wanted to do, but he wasn't going to back down. That afternoon, Big Mike stood on the tracks waiting for Jay, but Jay never showed up. All the boys and Arthur's cousins chased Big Mike—there must have been about eight or nine of them, but three or four of the cousins began beating on Big Mike.

The next day at school, the rumor about the beating that Big Mike took from all those boys spread, and Jay wanted nothing to do with fighting Big Mike.

Big Mike finished third and fourth grade at that school, then his mom and dad moved him back across town.

Now in fifth grade, Big Mike was back at his old school. He immediately began looking for Carol, but she was no longer there. But Arthur was.

Big Mike started wearing a patch over his left eye to try to make the right eye stronger from not wearing his glasses for two years. At school, some kids were picking on Arthur about Big Mike —they had been picking on him from the first grade all the way to the fifth grade. It was more than Arthur could handle. One day, while walking to music class, Big Mike started to laugh along with them, and before he knew it, Arthur punched him in the eye. Big Mike never saw it coming. It was hard, fast, and over before he knew it. Luckily for Big Mike, Arthur only hit him once.

After that day, Big Mike never wore the patch again. Because of this, his eye was permently damaged, from bullying and Big Mike's pride, since he didn't want to wear the patch.

Big Mike had a hard time adjusting to his school work, so he failed the fifth grade. He spent the next year being the biggest kid in school, since he had failed the previous year. When Big Mike was signing himself into his middle school, they asked him what grade he was in. Big Mike lied and said seventh, so he could be in the same grade as his friends. He never saw the sixth grade or knew the work.

So Big Mike became the class clown, spending three years in seventh grade. On his third year, he was kicked out for behavioral issues for the rest of the year and had a court date. On the date of court, the judge made an example out of him; they pulled the divider wall open in the court room, and there was Big Mike's entire class, watching him be sentenced to a detention center.

Big Mike arrived in detention, where he would stay in a dorm with about eighty kids—two to each room, except one room had about ten beds in it. When they placed Big Mike in there, to his surprise, he saw five or six boys from the rough side of town who he knew from third grade. His experiences with bullying started all over again. After a couple of months, he was shipped home, but he wasn't allowed to attend public school, so his mom and dad had to place him in private school. Big Mike dropped out when he turned sixteen, and he never saw high school again.

17

THE DAY MIKE'S BEST FRIEND, BUCK, DIED

Big Mike continued his journey through life but learned how to fight and win. There was a challenge at a local bar called a "Bad Man" contest. The winner would take home $500. Big Mike was not a drinker, but from time to time, he would have a shot to warm himself up before fighting.

Big Mike had a dog named Buck. Buck was a massive pit bull and the biggest, strongest, craziest dog ever. When Big Mike had gotten him, Buck was already grown and set in his ways. No one could tame or get close to him other than Big Mike. Buck was well known as a fighter with a winning track record, but when Big Mike got him, Big Mike tried to put that life of fighting behind him. Buck was always on a twenty-foot logging chain tied to concrete blocks. It wasn't the life Big Mike wanted for his dog, but Buck was too dangerous to run free.

One day, Big Mike was in his house eating when he heard Buck going crazy. He ran outside to see what was going on and saw that a truck had pulled into his yard. It was Arthur and his cousins; they knew the dog from the previous owner and had come looking for him uninvited. With their truck backed up into the driveway, they lowered the tailgate and let out a big pit bull. The dog ran toward Buck with teeth that could kill. Even though he was on a chain, Buck nearly killed their dog. Before Big Mike knew what was going on, they quickly grabbed their injured dog and spun out of the driveway.

Big Mike always walked Buck and would take him everywhere. Buck especially liked riding in the back of Big Mike's Jeep. One late night, while riding home from the store, Big Mike noticed a truck following him. After turning down street after street, there were now two then three cars following him. He turned into a backyard to cut across streets, trying to get away, but there was no way out, and more cars came. They all circled Big Mike's Jeep with their headlights blinding him; there must have been about twenty to thirty people in around eight to ten cars by now. Big Mike got out of the Jeep with Buck in the back, hooked to his logging chain. Big Mike could hear dogs growling like crazy. Buck started barking and snapping his jaws, then he heard someone say, "You better get your dog out because mine is going to kill it."

Big Mike said, "No." Then from about thirty to forty feet away, a dog was running straight at Big Mike. As the dog approached the front of the Jeep and was seconds from attacking, Buck jumped out on top of the dog, ripping and tearing it to pieces. Big Mike grabbing Buck's chain and pulled it, yelling, "Stop it!" He looked up and saw three more dogs turned loose, making a total of four dogs running toward him, with Buck still on a chain. Big Mike thought for sure this was going to be the end of Buck.

Buck kept fighting for what seemed like twenty minutes. He destroyed one dog after another, killing a couple and making the others run away. Buck also saved Big Mike's life, as everyone jumped into their cars and ran away from Buck, who was jumping after everyone, keeping them away from Big Mike. Big Mike got Buck back into his Jeep and went a home a winner.

A few days later, Big Mike went out to feed Buck, and he found that someone had killed Buck with poisoned meat. Big Mike knew who it was and why. He was sad, for he had lost his best friend. Buck died on a Friday, and Big Mike went out that night to a new contest. He was always fighting the "Bad Man" contest, which was a popular thing at that time. The contest was held all over town in different bars, featuring different fighters. However, Big Mike had no plans to fight that night.

As he walked in the bar, the bouncers and a lot of people there knew Big Mike, and they asked him if he was there to fight. Big Mike said, "No, just checking it out," as he made his way to the ring side. He saw a friend there named Billy. Billy was a big boy but had a heart of gold; there wasn't a fighting bone in his body, but he could scare you with his looks and voice.

The fights were supposed to start at 9:00 p.m., but it was 9:45 p.m., and nothing was going on. Then, across the PA, Big Mike heard a request. "Does anybody want to fight? We have no one wanting to fight our champion." Looking around, Big Mike saw about two hundred people, and many were big guys. *Why is no one fighting?* Big Mike thought.

Then he heard it again. "Does anyone want to fight Buck?" Big Mike couldn't believe his ears.

"Did they say 'Buck'?" he asked Billy.

"Yes," Billy said. "No one can beat him."

Big Mike felt that Buck was somehow calling him from the grave. He stepped up and said, "I will fight him. Where is he at?"

Everyone looked at him, thinking he was joking. Big Mike asked again. "Where is he at?"

Then the announcer said, "We have a fighter!"

They took Big Mike back to the dressing room behind the bar and kitchen, with Billy following them, saying, "Hold on! They must go get him. He is next door at the gym."

The bar was located at a plaza shopping center, and someone went out to call Buck backstage. This was the first time Big Mike saw Buck, as he looked down the hallway with his back turned away from Big Mike, wearing a red robe with gold letters that said "Buck." When Buck dropped his robe, Big Mike saw that Buck was three times his size, and he was jumping rope.

Big Mike always wore blue jeans; he never dressed out to fight. They asked him if there was anything he needed before the match. "I will take two shots of tequila," Big Mike said. Keep in mind, he was not a drinker, and all the other times, even if he had a shot, it was always one, not two. This fight was different, for Big Mike's heart was in it. Also, the stage was up higher and closer to the lights than all the rest of the stages he had fought on. The song "Rocky" was on as Big Mike entered the stage. He never thought twice about the fight; he just went out swinging to the sound of the bell.

The three-minute rounds felt like three seconds at first. When the bell rang at the end of the first round, Buck and Big Mike didn't stop fighting; they went right through the first round into the second.

The crowd went crazy, cheering like never before. The second bell rang, and they kept fighting. The people had to pull them apart. As Big Mike went to his corner, Billy was still on the ground. People were yelling at Billy, saying, "Give your man some water!" Big Mike could see the fear on Billy's face as he climbed up the ring side to give him water.

"Ding, ding!" they were off fighting again, and by this time, the rounds felt like they were fifteen minutes long. Now, Big Mike was taking hits so hard that he felt like he was in a pillow fight—he couldn't feel pain, but he could hear some of the crowd saying he was going to get brain damage.

Buck was so strong, but Big Mike never gave up finishing all the rounds. The fight ended in a tie. Big Mike wasn't fighting for the money or contest; he was fighting for Buck. No one knew Big Mike had lost his dog that day.

Big Mike went on fighting place after place, knocking them out and winning in the first and second round. Then, one day, the fight was at a local place. Mike was fighting the Florida

State kickboxer, and in his competitor's corner were Arthur and many others. Big Mike finished off one after another; he was supposed to only fight one that week and move on, but he beat everyone who accepted his challenge that night.

No one ever intimidated Big Mike ever again. Big Mike moved on to many other challenges of all types, setting and holding world records, from car lifting to bolder tossing to firetruck pulling. He beat everyone who crossed his path. His nickname was Giant Killer. Big Mike held his spot at the top until he, his mom, and his dad were in a car accident, leaving Mike with TBI, all alone.

18

BIG MIKE'S NIGHTMARES

Big Mike found himself dreaming more and more, but his dreams consisted mostly of him crossing a bridge on a rainy day, then experiencing an accident. In each dream, he received more and more information. Big Mike brushed it off.

One day at Linda's house, Big Mike was watching TV with Chris. It was a rainy day, and he fell asleep in the recliner chair as Linda was cooking dinner for them and Mary was out showing property. All of a sudden, Big Mike jumped halfway out of his chair, scaring Linda. "What's wrong?!" Linda shouted.

"Oh, nothing. It's just a dream," Big Mike answered.

"A dream?" Linda asked.

"Yes. I have been having the same dream for a few months now, and it's not a good one."

"What is it about?"

"I can't explain it," Big Mike answered. "I'm just riding in a car or a truck—I'm not sure—but each time I have the dream, I get more and more information." Big Mike paused, trying to collect his thoughts. "I'm riding in a storm and crossing a bridge, then suddenly, something hits me from behind, and I'm flying in the air. That was the first one, then there was another one, which was worse. I woke up in the dream, and the vehicle I was in was under water. It was filling up with water, and I knew I was going to drown. But then I woke up. A few months later, the same dream came for the third time. But this time, I was flying over a bridge before hitting the bottom. As I was looking down, I saw trees and a river of fast-running water, but looking up into the clouds, I saw that they were black and scary. I was not afraid, because there was one big cloud of light above them all. I was flying into it. I can only imagine it was heaven. Then I woke up. Crazy dream, isn't it, Mom?"

"Yes, it is, son," Linda said, "But remember, it's just a dream." Linda was wondering about Big Mike's car accident with his mom and dad. She worried that he was starting to dream and remember his past but just couldn't connect the dots. Still, his past was not as important as his future with Chris and Mary. Finally, life for Big Mike was good.

19

THE LETTER

Mary did not feel the love she was hoping Big Mike would remember they had. She would often stop at the park down the street from their house, where she and Ricky had made a lot of memories. She would let Chris play while she read letters from Ricky when he was off at war. She always carried the last letter in her purse, and when she felt alone, she would go to the park and read it. Now that Ricky was home and she still felt alone, she knew something just wasn't right.

Sitting on the bench by a small pond, Mary pulled out the last letter. Before reading it, she said, "God, I know You're probably not happy with the way I talked to You the day I got the news about Ricky, but I'm sorry. I never stopped believing in You. I was just mad at You, and all these years, I thought that if I didn't talk to You or go to church, somehow, I would be paying You back for the way You let my life go. When I gave my life to You, Lord, I expected everything to be ok, that it would go smooth. When my life was not changed for the better, I felt lied to. Lord, I don't want to go through it alone anymore. Please forgive me. Come back into my life again. I need You. God, only You can bring me happiness again."

As Mary felt the heat from the sunlight drying the tears on her face, she believed that God had answered her prayers in some way. She opened the letter and started to read it.

Dear Rosebud,

It's your Stud Muffin again. My thoughts of you today are of the first time we got these names. You probably gave me mine because I was eating a little too much and putting on a few extra pounds around the waist. Those pounds weren't there when we met, and you thought of me as your muffin—sweet and special—and you knew I was a stud, lol.

I know I never told you why I called you Rosebud, so you probably thought it was because of all the roses I gave you. Well, let me tell you something: the rosebud is the flower that hasn't opened yet. When we first met, you were young and hadn't opened your heart to anyone else—only me. I knew it. I kept it with me all the days of my life, even today. My little rosebud has bloomed. She has become a mother, a wonderful wife, and my best friend. I daydream back to the flower from time to time, and I wish I could have made different choices in life, like not leaving you alone so much. I hope and pray—yes, "pray"—that God gives us extra time on this earth to make up for the lost time. I may not be close to you right now like you want, but remember this letter when you're thirsty and need to be watered.

Love,
Stud Muffin

PS: Tell our son, Chris, that I will be home soon and will finally get to meet him.

After Mary found relief in reading Ricky's last letter, she made her way back home, knowing that something would be different this time.

20

RICKY'S CHILDHOOD TREE FORT

One day, Big Mike and Mary were out shopping in their home town of Winter Garden, FL, and they entered a small diner—one that the parents of Ricky's best friend, Tim, had owned for over forty years. The food recipes had been passed down from their grandmother, who opened the diner with the savings she had earned from when she was a child selling cookies. She was always dreaming one day of having her own kitchen. She said that when she was a little girl, her mom and dad lived on a wagon and never had a place to sit down and eat, always moving from town to town and helping others wherever they would stop. On the road, she would help her mother serve breakfast for her dad and four brothers. The family of seven would have to take turns using the plates, as they only had a set of four.

Tim was small. They called him Little Tim or Tiny Tim for laughs, but there was nothing small about his heart. It was probably the biggest heart this small town had ever seen. Tim had taken over the diner, and every Wednesday, the food was free. It was a sight to see. On Sunday after church, Tim would open up the sidewalks in front of the diner and the diner's outdoor patio, and every person in town seemed to come. Tim's diner was a donation "free" diner that served lunch all day. No one would go home hungry, not even the homeless.

This day was the first time Tim had seen his friend Ricky since they were kids. They had first met in the woods playing with other kids. The kids would all build forts in trees or dig holes in the side of the banks where the river would run. They probably had about ten tree forts all over the edge of town, but the best fort was three stories tall. The older kids had built it, and it was abandoned. Everyone knew about it, and the only way up was to climb a knotted rope in the center of the room on each floor. You had to be strong to climb—no girls or wimps allowed.

One day, Ricky was on the third floor and the other kids from town were at the bottom of the tree. The talk was about who could make it to the top—kind of like king of the mountain. Everyone picked on Tiny Tim, saying, "You can't do it! You are too small." That was all it took for Tiny Tim—he was off before anyone knew it.

He scaled right up those ropes, probably the fastest he had ever climbed. All the kids were saying, "Tim is faster than Ricky!" This was how Tim and Ricky met. The other kids made a challenge to see who could climb up the big rope the fastest. Ricky was surprised to see the big rope was outside the window; it went from the third floor to probably twenty feet further up to the tree top, where there was a small platform to look out. No one had ever seen anyone go up there; it was probably the oldest part of the fort. The older kids must have put it there years ago.

Ricky was just about to say "No way" when little Tim said, "Ok, Ricky first." Ricky was not one to back down from a challenge, even if he did not want to do it or if he was afraid.

So out the third floor window and up the rope he went, never looking down. He climbed up with relief, saying, "I made it!" as the kids counted to 115.

Tim said, "No problem," and off he went as the kids counted to 92. Tim made it—he beat Ricky.

But Ricky was not a sore loser. "Good job, buddy," he said as they grabbed each other's hands with their thumbs overlocking each other. Tim felt the strength in Ricky's grip. Ricky was stronger, but Tim was lighter and faster.

As they looked out around, they could see the town's water tower; they appeared to be higher than it. The wood platform they were standing on was old and in need of repair, and they both knew it was probably not made for two people.

"We'd better get down," Ricky said.

"Yeah," Tim said without fear, for he was the winner.

As Tim started down first, he was just clearing his head from the bottom of Ricky's feet when he saw that he had over twenty feet to go. Ricky looked up to see the rope was being cut from the branch above. Tim was past the point of return. Ricky laid down on the platform, wrapping his arm and wrist around the rope just in time, then...snap! The rope broke. Ricky was holding all of Tim's weight with one arm, while his other arm was holding the wooden platform to keep himself from being pulled off.

When Tim felt the small drop, he looked up to see Ricky's arm holding his life. It was bleeding badly from the rope cutting into it. Tim had a long way to go and tried not to shake much.

The kids below were screaming. What had taken a minute to climb up felt like an eternity to get down, then Tim finally reached the third floor. Ricky pulled up the rope, tying off the broken part, and began making his way down safely, but the rope burned around his wrists and hands. The burns were so deep, they would last forever.

As Big Mike and Mary were seated at the diner, Tim noticed them. He came up and said, "Hi, Ricky! It's been a long time."

Big Mike reached out to shake Tim's hand. Tim notice that the scar was not on Ricky's hand. He knew all about Ricky's recovery and how he was a hero in this town. Their childhood tree day happened before Ricky met Mary, so Tim did not mention it to Mary. "Dinner is on me," he said.

As Mary and Big Mike were leaving the restaurant, Big Mike was holding the door for Mary to exit. At the same time, a man on the sidewalk began walking faster, thinking that Mike was holding the door for him. The man entered, running right into Mary. To Mary's surprise, it was John. John was just as surprised.

John was a man Mary had dated when Ricky was in the hospital. Mary had told John that she had to end their relationship due to her work schedule and because she needed time with Chris, who had health issues, which was a lie. The only one in her family with health issues was her husband, Ricky, who had woken up. One time, John had asked Mary about Chris's dad, and Mary said that he was lost at war. John had never questioned it until today.

"Excuse me. I'm sorry," John said.

Mary looked up, at a loss for words. "It's ok," she said.

Still holding the door, Big Mike stared at them. Both John and Mary looked at him at the same time.

"This is my husband, Ricky," Mary said.

As John's heart skipped a beat, he reached out to shake Big Mike's hand. "Nice to meet you," he said.

"You too," said Big Mike.

John and Big Mike continued staring at each other. All three of them had stepped outside onto the sidewalk, and the door closed behind them. Big Mike seemed to recall that familiar face.

"Do I know you from somewhere?" he asked.

With a scared look on his face, John stuttered, "No, No. I don't think so." He did, however, remember Big Mike.

John was the paramedic firefighter who was driving the ambulance when Big Mike had his accident and lost his mom and dad. John knew this, and he was very confused from the story Mary had told him. Things just didn't add up.

Mary looked just as scared, although she knew nothing about Big Mike and John and the day of the accident. "Well, we must be going," she said. "It's good to see you again."

"You too," said John.

═══ 21 ═══

MARY HAS A SURPRISE

Some time had passed, and Mary and Big Mike had been doing well. Mary had a surprise for Big Mike. She was pregnant and had plans to show Big Mike a house she had picked out only a few blocks away from their current home. This house had an extra room for their new baby. Mary had set up two rooms to show Big Mike: a boy's room with a red firetruck and a red balloon in the middle of the empty room, and a girl's room with a pink balloon attached to a pink stroller. At this point, Mary did not know if her baby was a boy or a girl, and no one even knew she was pregnant.

One Saturday morning, Mary told Big Mike she needed his help to stage a house before noon. He had no idea he was going to their

Mary Has A Surprise

new house. As they made their way into the house, Big Mike said, "Wow, this is nice! It has a pool and a backyard that sits on a lake." He was amazed.

Then with Mary behind him, Big Mike opened the bedroom door—it was the boy's room. Big Mike quickly turned around and looked at Mary's belly. "Are…are you?!" he stuttered.

"Yes!" Mary said. "But I don't know if this room is good."

"Why not?" Big Mike asked. After looking at the door Mary was pointing to, he finally opened it—it was the girl's room.

"What? Twins?"

"Oh, no, no. Just one," Mary answered. "But I'm not going to find out if it is a boy or a girl. I want it to be a surprise."

Big Mike was crying. He began hugging and kissing Mary, then he slowly made his way down to his knees, kissing Mary's belly. In soft words, Big Mike thanked God for this day and then told Mary, "This is a day I will never forget." He then asked what time the people were coming to see the house.

Mary laughed. "They are already here!"

"What...what do you mean?" Big Mike asked. "This is our new home."

Big Mike shouted with excitement. "We must go tell Linda and Chris!" he exclaimed.

"No, not today. This is our day," Mary said.

She and Big Mike walked out back to enjoy the moment by the lake.

22

MARY GOES INTO LABOR

On a Monday morning, Mary was seven months pregnant and was unloading boxes from her car at the new house when a sharp pain came across her lower abdominal. She dropped a box to the ground and noticed she was bleeding badly. She called 911 and was rushed to the hospital.

Linda, Chris, and Big Mike had no idea that Mary was in the emergency room. Mary gave birth to a boy, and her baby needed blood; however, Mary couldn't give it because of the complications with labor. She told the doctors, "Please call my husband, Ricky." The doctors took down all the information and pulled up Ricky's records.

While waiting for Ricky and Linda to arrive, the doctors came back to Mary to tell her that Ricky's blood type did not match the baby. Asking how this could be, Mary wondered how her child would get the blood. As Linda walked into the emergency room, she saw Mary, who was crying. Linda rushed over to her side.

"What is the matter?" she asked.

"Ricky's blood does not match the baby's, and that is impossible," Mary cried. Linda began to panic, thinking she had just been caught in the lie she had been living.

"What do you mean?!" she asked.

Mary replied, "The records they have on file show that Ricky's blood type does not match!"

When Big Mike arrived at the hospital, the doctors took his blood and said it was a match. One of the doctors told Mary, "I'm sorry for the confusion. The military must have written his blood type incorrectly."

Linda gave a big sigh of relief and thought to herself, *I can continue my lie.*

23

THE TRUTH

After a few years had passed, Linda had still not recorded any of the videos of the new baby, named Ricky the Third. The real Ricky, who was in the basement, had no idea there was a new baby in the family.

Linda's eyesight was beginning to fade, and since she was becoming blind, she was not able to drive or leave home much. She didn't know how long she could live this lie.

She began to cry and pray, "God, help me. I can't take care of my son anymore." Crying harder, she prayed, "Help me soon, God. Please help me."

Linda decided to write a letter to explain what she had done, knowing that if she didn't write it soon, she may not be able to see well enough to write. She finished the letter and placed it into her hope chest at the foot of her bed with still no answer about how to get out of her lie.

Chris was now twenty years old. He had spent the last two years since graduation telling his mom he was waiting for a college to accept him, but the truth was that he had enlisted into the army.

It had been some time since Big Mike and Mary had their baby, and Big Mike had a made a remarkable recovery. He had even been driving a car for over a year.

One Friday afternoon, before Christmas weekend, Big Mike took Linda to the eye doctor alone. It was raining, and the roads were wet. As they were crossing a bridge on the outside of town, a truck came from behind without seeing them. Big Mike slowed down to cross the bridge, but the truck hit his car, running Big Mike and Linda off the bridge and into the river below. They both began drowning, just like in Big Mike's nightmare.

The news reached Mary and Chris, and they were broken. Life had stopped for them, and there was no tomorrow. That Saturday, which was Christmas Eve, passed in the blink of an eye.

On Christmas Day, Mary received a call. It was the chief of police, and he was very sorry for calling her on Christmas. He told Mary he need paperwork by Monday to complete the investigation.

That afternoon, Mary and Chris went over to Linda's house to look for a birth certificate and paperwork for Ricky, who was really Big Mike. After Chris broke the lock from his grandma's hope chest, he found the letter. He and Mary read page after page of Linda's letter of all the lies, yet the love Linda had while trying to save Chris and Mary from pain made them somewhat understand.

The last letter had no ending to it. It was blank and had been dated three days before. On top of Linda's last letter was a set of keys for the basement.

Mary and Chris made their way to the basement door and down the stairs. Ricky was sitting in a chair, watching a movie that had been playing over and over. As he stood up, he turned around and said, "My son."

Chris was standing still, frozen in his tracks as Mary walked up from a distance. She knew everything. With tears in her eyes, she opened her arms for a hug. Ricky, knowing nothing, opened his arms and gave her that special hug…bump, bump, bam.

Ricky had no memories, only the movies that he had lived all those years upstairs. Mary had been starting to live her own lie, and not knowing how to explain the new baby and what had just happened, the lie continued.

24

Evening News Report

World news reports that a man who has been missing for over thirty years was found on a life raft off the coast of North Atlantic Ocean and placed in a rehab hospital in Africa. His estimated age and name is unknown due to TBI (traumatic brain injury). Doctor reports say the only object to identify him was a ripped shirt that had a half-torn name tag saying "Ricky Sr."

And that's all for the world news tonight. Have a great night.

www.ingramcontent.com/pod-product-compliance
Ingram Content Group UK Ltd.
Pitfield, Milton Keynes, MK11 3LW, UK
UKHW041955230426
12048UKWH00008B/344